Some people said it would never happen. They said the littlest sister couldn't do it. And yet . . .

For my little family—Mom, Dad, Jeff, and Gabriel—and for all
the littlest girls and boys reaching for their big dreams.
— K. G.

For Jjaja Margaret Monica Ntwatwa Walabyeki and
Grandma Adline Mgbakwa Onyenamereibeya Ahanonu.
— M. A.

First published in 2019 by Page Street Kids,
an imprint of
Page Street Publishing Co.
27 Congress Street, Suite 105
Salem, MA 01970
www.pagestreetpublishing.com

Distributed by Macmillan, sales in Canada by
The Canadian Manda Group

19 20 21 22 23 CCO 5 4 3 2 1

ISBN-13: 978-1-62414-694-7

ISBN-10: 1-62414-694-5

CIP data for this book is available from the Library of Congress.

This book was typeset in Museo Slab.
The illustrations were done in Illustrator.

Printed and bound in Shenzhen, Guangdong, China

Page Street Publishing uses only materials from suppliers who are committed to
responsible and sustainable forest management.

Page Street Publishing protects our planet by donating to nonprofits like The Trustees,
which focuses on local land conservation.

SERENA
THE LITTLEST SISTER

Karlin Gray

illustrated by **Monica Ahanonu**

PAGE
STREET
KiDS

Serena stood in Arthur Ashe Stadium and kissed the trophy. The crowd roared. Her parents took pictures. Her sisters cheered.

Thirteen years earlier, four-year-old Serena jumped out of
the family van in Compton, California, and followed her sisters:

big sister, **VENUS**;

big, big sister, **LYNDREA**;

big, big, big sister, **ISHA**;

and big, big, big, big sister, **YETUNDE**.

Running past the playground and onto the public tennis courts, the girls pushed a shopping cart full of balls and carried rackets and brooms. Once cleaned, the courts were ready for the girls to practice.

"Look at the ball, Serena,"
her father coached.
"Just swing."

Using an adult-size racket, Serena swung again and again.
Her sisters cheered when Serena hit the ball . . . and they chased
the ones she missed.

Their father taught Serena and her sisters how to play tennis.
He read books and watched videos, received donated equipment
from tennis clubs, and made the sport a family activity.

Because the donated balls were old, many had lost their bounce. But they used them anyway, after their father explained that it was good practice for Wimbledon—a Grand Slam tournament where the balls bounced lower because the tennis court was made of grass.

And on special days, when they opened a new can of balls, the girls couldn't wait to smack them.

Pock!

Pock!

Pock!

At home, the girls made up a box-ball game called "Grand Slam"—named after the four most important tennis competitions in the world. Serena and her sisters used their hands to hit a ball back and forth on sidewalk squares, pretending they were playing at the US Open or the Australian Open.

If they wanted to play the lawn courts of Wimbledon, they sprinkled grass on the squares. If they wanted to play the clay courts of the French Open, they scattered dirt.

Serena loved winning their Grand Slams because, well, Serena loved being the star.

When Lyn wrote plays for the girls to perform, Serena always played the princess.

When Tunde and Isha experimented with new fashion looks, Serena modeled their designs.

And when they all played card games, Serena declared herself the winner . . . even if she didn't actually win.

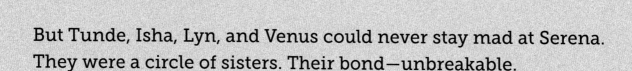

But Tunde, Isha, Lyn, and Venus could never stay mad at Serena. They were a circle of sisters. Their bond—unbreakable.

In the evenings, all five sisters slept in one bedroom with two sets of bunk beds. Isha and Tunde were on the top beds, Lyn and Venus on the bottom beds. And little Serena wiggled in with a different sister each night.

Over the years, their dad put up inspirational signs around
the tennis court. They were never allowed to use the word *can't*.

And their mom often told them, "Whatever you become, you become in your head first." So the girls dreamed of what they could become:

Tunde, a nurse . . .

Isha, a lawyer . . .

Lyn, a singer . . .

and Venus and Serena, #1 tennis players.

All the sisters liked tennis, but Venus hit harder, ran faster, and won. Reporters, coaches, and famous tennis players started to notice—especially when they saw her serve a ball at 100 miles per hour!

"Daddy," Serena pleaded, "give me a chance. I want to play in tournaments like V."

"Not yet," her father said. "You're not ready."

But one day, eight-year-old Serena got an idea while playing "office" with her sisters. As they pretended to answer phones and shuffle papers, Serena spotted an application for one of Venus's tournaments. Serena quietly filled it out and mailed it.

At the event, the girls' parents watched Venus compete on one court while Serena sneaked off to another.

As Serena played her first match, her plan was simple: exhaust her opponent by running her all over the court. Her strategy worked, and Serena won the match!

Then her father appeared at the back of the crowd.

Serena prepared herself for punishment. Instead of being angry, her dad exclaimed, "Look at you! You won! You played great!" Then he started coaching her on how to play her next opponent.

"You really think I can beat her?" Serena asked.

Her dad assured her, "You can do anything."

Serena won all her matches, moving up and up until . . .

she faced her big sister in the final match. In the changeovers, Serena whispered, "Venus, let me win a game."

Ten-year-old Venus ignored Serena and easily won the gold trophy.

Although Serena left with silver, she kept eyeing that gold.

"You know what?" Venus asked. "I've always liked silver better than gold. You want to trade?"

Serena cherished that trophy. She always wanted to be like all her sisters, especially Venus.

If Venus went somewhere, Serena followed. If they ate in restaurants, Serena ordered the same meal as Venus. And after Venus told a reporter, "I want to win Wimbledon," Serena said the exact same thing: "I want to win Wimbledon."

Her father told her, "You're your own person, Serena. You don't have to do everything Venus does."

The next time a reporter asked, Serena said, "I want to win the US Open."

But she still loved to copy Venus.

Other people, however, didn't think Serena was as talented as her sister. One newspaper article claimed Serena would never be as successful as Venus because younger siblings never go very far in sports.

Tunde took Serena aside. "Don't pay any attention to that article, Serena. You'll have your day. And it's gonna be even bigger."

Serena kept Tunde's words close to her heart.

After a few years of tournaments, the Williams family moved to Florida, where Isha, Lyn, Venus, and Serena attended a tennis academy. Tunde stayed in California to go to nursing school. The sisters didn't like being separated, but their new life in Florida kept them busy with schoolwork and plenty of tennis.

Here, the girls didn't sweep the courts. There were brand-new rackets and unopened cans of balls!

Many kids wore stylish tennis outfits, but none wore beaded braids like Serena and her sisters. The girls from Compton stood out on these courts . . .

but so did their powerful strokes.

Pock!

Pock!

Pock!

When Venus turned fourteen, she was allowed to play in professional tournaments—events where the prizes were big checks! And in her first match, Venus won.

A year and a half later, Serena turned pro at fourteen, like Venus. But unlike Venus, Serena lost.

So Venus and Serena started playing as a doubles team. Playing with her sister, Serena felt stronger. Their motto was, "If you can't do it for you, do it for me."

By the time she turned sixteen, Serena had grown taller and more confident. She was ready to play on her own—and in her own style.

Serena wasn't as strong or as fast as Venus, so she angled her shots to win. After she fell off her skateboard one day, it hurt her wrist too much to hit a backhand. Instead, Serena ran around the ball and hit her forehand extra hard.

Serena and Venus traveled the world—competing as a doubles team and against each other. Whenever Serena and Venus played against each other in Grand Slams, the press called it a "Sister Slam." But for the sisters, every "slam" ended with a hug.

And at the 1999 French Open Doubles competition, seventeen-year-old Serena and eighteen-year-old Venus won their first Grand Slam together.

Before Serena's eighteenth birthday, she and Venus competed in the US Open—the tournament Serena dreamed of winning. Her big sister Venus was a favorite to win, but to the crowd's surprise, Venus lost.

It was Serena who won match . . . after match . . . after match.

When she reached the finals, she faced the player who had knocked Venus out of the tournament.

"Now she's playing for two people," Venus said, as she watched from the stands above.

This was the moment Serena had been training for since she was a little girl in Compton. *I gotta go for it*, Serena told herself.

Pock!

Pock!

Pock!

She smashed eight aces— serves that her opponent couldn't even touch. And her fierce forehand earned her point after point.

In the end, Serena won the tournament and became the first black woman to win a Grand Slam singles tournament in more than forty years.

Tunde had been right: "You'll have your day. And it's gonna be even bigger."

At the awards ceremony, Serena looked up at her family. "I would like to also thank my dad, my mom," she said, "and all my sisters for all the support."

Serena held the trophy up high as the loudspeaker boomed, "Ladies and gentlemen, the 1999 US Open Women's Singles champion—Serena Williams."

The crowd roared.

Photographers flashed photos.

And one of the many headlines of the day read,

Little Sister, BIG HIT!

AFTERWORD

"The greatest love of all? At first, it was my family. My sisters."
—Serena Williams

On September 11, 1999, Serena Williams became the first black woman to win the US Open since Althea Gibson's victory in 1957. The next day, Serena and Venus won the US Open Women's Doubles trophy together. Venus's childhood dream also came true in 2000 when she won Wimbledon. Afterward, Venus told her mom, "Serena showed me how to win."

As sisters, Serena and Venus made history: They were the first sisters to win Olympic gold medals in doubles tennis (2000 Olympic Games); they were the first sisters to both win Grand Slam singles titles individually (Serena in 1999 US Open and Venus in 2000 Wimbledon); and they were the first sisters to have a Career Doubles Golden Slam—winning an Olympic gold medal in doubles and all four majors in doubles.

In 2017, Serena and Venus played against each other in the Australian Open. When Serena won, she made history again—setting a record for the most major titles in the Open era. Thirty-five-year-old Serena said, "I really would like to take this moment to congratulate Venus. [. . .] She is my inspiration. There's no way I would be at 23 [titles] without her. There is no way I would be at one without her. Thank you, Venus, for inspiring me to be the best player I could be and inspiring me to work hard."

"Even when Serena beats me, I sometimes pull out my camera and take pictures of her on the victory stand. Nothing can keep me from celebrating when my best friend wins a match."
—Venus Williams

"I think it is one of the greatest things in the world to have sisters."
—Isha Price

SERENA AND HER FAMILY

SERENA grew up to be ranked a #1 tennis player who won more Grand Slam titles than any other tennis player—male or female. She is an Olympic gold medalist and was named the 2015 *Sports Illustrated* Sportsperson of the Year. One of the highest-paid female athletes, Serena started her own fashion line and has performed in TV and film.

"At the end of the day, we're always looking out for other people. . . . We're supposed to look out for each other because we should learn from each other."
—Lyndrea Price

VENUS also grew up to be ranked a #1 tennis player and an Olympic gold medalist. She helped win the fight for equal prize money for women and men at Wimbledon, broke the record for the fastest serve in women's tennis (129 miles per hour!), and created her own fashion line and interior design company.

LYNDREA played tennis in college and has worked in web design, songwriting, and fashion merchandising.

ISHA also played tennis in college and went to law school. Today she is a lawyer who works closely with her sisters.

TUNDE grew up to be a nurse like their mom. Tragically, Tunde passed away in 2003. To honor her, Serena and her family opened the Yetunde Price Resource Center in Compton, California.

RICHARD WILLIAMS and **ORACENE PRICE** were their daughters' first coaches. Although they divorced in 2002, they raised all their girls to be part of a strong sisterhood.

"We often get the question: 'So how does it feel to have famous sisters?' They're my sisters. . . . I still see them as Venus Williams, Serena Williams, not Venus Williams, tennis star, not Serena Williams, tennis star."
—Yetunde Price

BIBLIOGRAPHY

BOOKS

Edmondson, Jacqueline. *Venus and Serena Williams: A Biography*. Westport, CT: Greenwood Press, 2005.

Williams, Serena, with Daniel Paisner. *On the Line*. New York: Grand Central Publishing, 2009. Direct quotes from this source on pages 8, 14, 16, 19, 21, 23, and 39.

———, and Venus Williams with Hilary Beard. *Venus and Serena:Serving from the Hip*. New York: Houghton Mifflin, 2005. Direct quotes from this source on pages 22 and 39.

———, and Venus Williams. *How to Play Tennis: Learn How to Play the Williams Sisters' Way*. New York: Dorling Kindersley, 2004.

Williams, Venus, with Kelly E. Carter. *Come to Win: Business Leaders, Artists, Doctors, and Other Visionaries on How Sports Can Help You Top Your Profession*. New York: Amistad, 2010. Direct quote from this source on page 14.

PERIODICALS

Associated Press, The. "Serena Williams Wins Open Record 23rd Grand Slam, Beats Sister Venus." *NBC Sports*, January 28, 2018. Direct quotes from this source on page 38.

Finn, Robin. "U.S. Open; Hingis Puts an End to the Williams' Sisters Act." *New York Times*, September 11, 1999. Direct quote from this source on page 35.

"Oprah Talks to Venus and Serena." *O, The Oprah Magazine*, March 2003.

Price, S. L. "Father Knew Best." *Sports Illustrated*, September 20, 1999. Direct quote from this source's cover on page 37.

———, "Slammin'." *Sports Illustrated*, September 9, 2014.

Roenigk, Alyssa. "Road to 23: The Story of Serena's Path to Greatness." espn.com, January 30, 2017. Direct quote from this source on page 20.

Steptoe, Sonja. "Child's Play." *Sports Illustrated*, June 10, 1991.

Sullivan, John Jeremiah. "Venus and Serena against the World." *New York Times Magazine*, August 23, 2012.

Wood, Gaby. "Serena Holds Court." *The Guardian*, May 5, 2007. Direct quote from this source on page 29.

FILM/TV

Venus and Serena: For Real. ABC Family, 2005.

Venus and Serena. Magnolia Home Entertainment, 2013. Direct quote from this source on page 35.

"Oprah Show." Harpo Entertainment, November, 27, 2002. Direct quotes from this source on page 39.

WEBSITES

1999 US Open footage: https://www.youtube.com/watch?v=KT7EzJ5ZMeY&app=desktop. Direct quotes from this source on page 37.

CNNSI.com: http://sportsillustrated.cnn.com/tennis/1999/us_open/news/1999/09/11/women_final_ap/.

Official website of Serena Williams: serenawilliams.com.

Official website of Venus Williams: venuswilliams.com.

Price, Lyndrea. Beyond the Baseline. By Jon Wertheim. *Sports Illustrated*, February 10, 2016. https://www.si.com/tennis/2016/02/11/pocast-lyndrea-price-venus-serena-williams. Direct quote from this source on page 39.